Joy Change

JUDY KENDALL

Cinnamon Press
Independent Innovative International

Published by Cinnamon Press
Meirion House, Glan yr afon, Tanygrisiau
Blaenau Ffestiniog, Gwynedd, LL41 3SU
www.cinnamonpress.com
The right of Judy Kendall to be identified as author of this work has been asserted by her in accordance with the Copyright, Designs and Patent Act, 1988. Copyright © 2010 Judy Kendall
ISBN: 978-1-907090-07-3
British Library Cataloguing in Publication Data. A CIP record for this book can be obtained from the British Library.

Designed and typeset in Palatino by Cinnamon Press. Cover design by Mike Fortune-Wood from original artwork 'Cherry Blossom' by Mike Hollmon and 'Moon' by billysview, agency © Dreamstime.com. Printed in Poland
Cinnamon Press is represented in the UK by Inpress Ltd www.inpressbooks.co.uk and in Wales by the Welsh Books Council www.cllc.org.uk.

Notes

The Small Country: In the 1860s the English Marines brought football to Japan—the first professional football league was established in 1993.

The Taihen Dancers: Taihen is the name of a Japanese group of dancers with disabilities.

The Most Beautiful: 'goldstream' is a possible reading of Kanazawa.

The First Fountain Ever Placed In A Japanese Garden: The first fountain was built in Kenroku en, Kanazawa, in 1861.

Cloud And Crane: 'to hammer down the peg that stands out'—a Japanese proverb.

Thanks

(I have angels for friends)
Chikako Murai and her father for a quiet writing space in their cafe; Iris Elgrichi and Eiko Miyaji for an inspiring foundation in Noh and haiku; Masuo Shioi for countless poetic discussions in the back of his antique shop
Kana Hayashi, Kana Oyabu and Rongmei Zhang for new perspectives on translation; Debbie Belardino, Hitomi Hyodo, Chie Kawabata, Beatrice Leroyer, Mary Ann Mooradian and Mieko Sawai for nourishment and practical support; and, last but not least, the alpine inspiration of Yukari Kimura and her family of mountaineers.

Also, the Lancaster eleven for humour and perceptive wit; Linda Anderson and Bill Herbert for being so demanding and encouraging (Lancaster University email MA in Creative Writing, 2000/01); Kanazawa University for giving me the time to write; Steve Earnshaw for work on the digital versions of some poems and Piers Messum for the title.

Acknowledgements

Thanks also to the journal editors who first published some of the poems in various versions and to the judges of poetry competitions who selected poems as winners and runners up, particularly to *Ambit, Asahi Shimbun, Birmingham & Midland Journal*, Wilkins Poetry Award, *Envoi, Equinox, Erbacce, European English Messenger, Fabric, Flash art Gallery, Haiku Quarterly, Iota, Indigo*, Capricorn Int'l poetry competition, Ludberg calendar 2008, MADBRIGHTON exhibition 2005, *North West Japanese Society Newsletter, Obsessed with Pipework, Orbis, Plum-line, PN Review, Presence, PROOF, Ragged Raven Anthology, Shamrock Haiku, Smiths Knoll, Stand & still* int'l haiku competitions. Also, Esqui Nouver Dance company and Kataribe Theatre group.
Brendan Kennelly, *Familiar Strangers: New & Selected Poems 1960-2004* (Bloodaxe Books, 2004). Used with kind permission.

Contents

Butterflies Spread Their Wings

Parts Of Kanazawa, And Beyond

Yes

for my parents

Kimono Colours

Heian period 794 - 1185

plum
willow tree
butterflies spreading their wings

wild pink
yellow day lily
Chinese vine

white oak
sea pine
bell clover

moon grass
cloud and crane
tiny bamboo

Butterflies Spread Their Wings

petals torn in the wind
how cold it is
waiting for the dawn

Wa, Harmony

The bell goes and I dismiss my class.
Tired and dishevelled, I start to pack away
my papers, wipe off chalk dust,
pack up the tape-deck when, *Teacher, sensei,*

a student hovers, polite, gentle, in need,
at an unobtrusive distance, offering me
a tremulous virgin face while he proceeds
in my hard language to mouth his soft apology

for missing last week's session
because he was unfortunately obliged
(oh teacher, hear out my confession)
to attend the funeral of his grandfather.

His English, slow and careful, broken,
he places in pieces on my gathered notes,
equidistant, partly as if in token
of his loss, partly in the hope

that I will read the spaces in between
the words of me and him, his duty
to the class, his unannounced departure, and fill in
the sadnesses to make consoling harmony,

but, sensing my tiredness and my need to get away
from school at this the end of a long day
and feeling shy, he leaves, and leaves me asking why
in my land we don't make young men this way.

in rain so heavy
with falling blossom, wishing
for you

Eye Of The Storm

Wheeling over Honshu, the largest island
on this three thousand kilometre stretch
of billowing ocean mountain-back,
split from the coast of a ravished Korea
(invasion, rape and pillage glossed over in Japan),
dusted by the inextricable unforgiving sand of China
(the Nanking rape, Manchurian
experimental camps erased):
They stole, the barbarians, China cries
our tea, calligraphy, religion.

Our tea, calligraphy, religion,
Japan replies *we rescued from barbarians*
and refined—without a thought
the crow swoops down, unerring,
towards the narrow coastal plains
of Noto, where fishermen daily sieve the seas of fish
and Kaga rice-growers scratch a sodden living,
towards Ishikawa, where some green remains
among the crops of houses,
where I live on the back side of Japan.

Where I live on the back side of Japan
the crow settles on a Kanazawa lamppost
beside the city hall, towards which the foreigners,
umbrellas blowing backwards, troop
to barter fingerprints for 'alien' IDs;
all save Koreans, whose victory comes
from laying to one side their shame
and stripping off their cloaks of local names
to claim their rights as victims. With such brave steps
relations should improve.

Relations should improve,
for here the coldest insult
is to be considered 'strange',
the worst of punishments
to be pushed out to perch,
shivering, in incessant rain.
Here where foreigners are known
as 'outside people'.
Like crows.
Never let in.

Never let in
to the inner circles,
fated to hover at Kanazawa castle gate,
scavenging leftovers,
liberated (mistakes expected, standards lowered),
from the rigours of politeness,
blessed with no shame.
Yet those that are wise exult in this permission to be odd,
accepting that to rip the mannered surface
will never take them to the quiet eye of the storm.

Oh Go

oh go
to the rain
to the fields of rice
stalks
where the wind blows
the scare crows
come
to the song
to the hill top
hey diddle

wouldn't you?
over there
two by two, my darling
come
the wishing well is
come

where the ground shakes
the earth quakes
and tea leaves scatter in the windy heights
around a room where no one
stops
to think of need
or you
my battered photograph
upon the door
that looks at me each time I go
to bring me back
tadaima

am I still your
other half or quarter or
what more is taken by another
as will be
as we both know
but no
relief
shortly upon the heels of next life's race
no breathing-space
no time off no
escape

wouldn't you
couldn't you
oh my shouldn't darling
come my

The Character Of Rain

'Gather yourself, we'll go into the cold'
—The Man Made Of Rain (Kennelly)

In Brendan Kennelly's vision a man
contains within him rain
and only rain,
just like the rei, the spirits of Japan,
built also from the character of rain.

It pours direct from heaven
when they open mouths to chant, sing, pray.
This is the weather-maker, the soothsayer's way—
words intended for gods, spoken by men
in possession of the spirits, of the rei.

The Small Country

in the English of Japanese university students

Japan is the small country
very small iseland
We lives in small house
and the road is narrow

Japanese economic condition is very bad
and the price of things are very high
We are bored in that condition
and we want someone to change it

Japan have four seasons
We have special feeling to cherry blossomes
We wear the yukata in summer
and we crazy about football only now

We have freedom and peace
Japan is very comfortable to live
and Mount Fuji is great view
However we tend to use a lot of things which we do not
realy need

Japan is small country and we are work hard every day
Many many people live in there
We have black hair, black eyes and eat raw fish
It is very beautiful

However Japanese is shy, Japanese is too shy

Foreigners

Foreigners are all the same,
exotic creatures
keen on noise.

Doughnut complexions,
and fiery tempers
when not dipped in saccharine.

They prefer flesh to fish.

Filled to capacity
with selfishness,
they look after their own
first. They do not think it wrong.

There is a distinct smell of old milk.

Their sugar levels are uncertain,
liable to explode.

And most of them possess
a careless flair
for turning the neatest room
into dishevelment.

They cannot gauge politeness,
their talents do not extend
to delicate matters.

Their women are loud,
noses mostly irresistible
and faces enviably unflat
(although they wrinkle early).

They cannot sit still
and have a tendency to wriggle.

A foreigner is always big.
You never see a small one.

The Crow's Nest

Cast adrift in a back alley
of this castle town (no castle now, burnt down),
I wait for a break in the buildings.

The dips between the concrete
are slippery, sliding off-centre
in uncertain directions,

and the streets
(where left is often right
back where I started

or where I never wished to go)
are fluid. Intended once to lose the enemy,
they now toss me, the friend,

from one lane to the next,
till Tokyu Hotel topples the skyline
and the banks crash in.

That night, at sundown,
when the streets rise up
and the moat fills with traffic,

the crows fly past in scores
to the derelict grounds that once held
a castle-military-camp-university

and now hold crows,
cawing momentary success,
all perches taken,

while I, washed up on a fifth floor balcony,
with its bird's eye view beyond the buildings,
find nothing to part me

from speckled waves of mountain,
but a few pebbles of concrete
and a few dots of crow.

Joy Change

I get an email from a friend
where he lets slip
the offer of a joy change—
just the thing
to lift the winter spirits,
greying in.

Later he sends again,
apologising.
He claims that he mistook,
late night, his fingers dripping type,
the y key for a b—
but they are miles apart.

He says he meant
a business teaching post
in foreign parts, with holidays,
lots of them, and pots
of money. It would be challenging—
he says.

It's all so in the clover,
falling in my lap,
to land upon my feet, steady, alone,
but oh how I'd been hoping
he would turn me on my head
less far from home.

Lost Communions

I Nihon, Japan

Sea sliding in on one side,
a mass of mountain pines upon the other,
I am squashed

but not alone—
living like others,
compressed in concrete,

save for occasional outings
to the low-lying peninsular
wilderness of Noto.

II Noto

One night in, I dip to sleep
amidst the sake-ridden shouts
of the mostly pensioned members

of Kanazawa City Climbing Club,
now gathered on a village green
to serenade the sky.

I wake, later, into a den of snores,
each telling a separate story
to the tatami straw: suu suu guusuka.

III Mamushi hill

Next day the group heads amiably towards a hill.
Mamushi says the sign perched on the slope:
a snake that jumps knee-high before it strikes,

a killer, quicker than the mukade centipede.
If bitten, best to back-track to the clinic
for you won't have much wild life left.

I prepare to panic
but my companions mock me, saying
mamushi snakes are rare these days and hardly ever seen.

IV Mamushi brow

Here, at the summit-marking stone,
instruction is imparted
ah sososo

as to which side is which
direction of the compass, such acumen acquired
not by knowing that moss makes for the north-side

but because some builder
has carved the corresponding
sign for kita on the stone.

V Kaeri return

Stop. Stop.
Look everyone. It's
apple blossom.

We all look.
But that is peach.
No, plum plum plum!

Doko? Where?
Petals shimmer all around.
Itaru tokoro ni, everywhere.

wafer-thin oblique
disdain as I lumber down
the parasoled lane

The ground is shifting.
You stray. I fray. Things scatter.
A tremor in the heart.

Parts Of Kanazawa, And Beyond

the Japanese character:
one signpost
so many different roads

The History Of The Parts of Kanazawa 金沢の歴

with thanks to Nelson's Japanese-English Character Dictionary for the readings of
'kana'/ '金', 'sawa' / '沢', and their respective compounds

I Kana 一 金

gold lines gold dust hush money　　　　　金線 金泥 金轡

gold embargo stone-deaf gold-tipped　　　金輸出禁止 金聾 金口

gold foil gold needle gold cord　　　　　金箔 金針 金水引

gold thread gold vein gold vessel　　　　金糸 金脈 金杯

fragrant olive *gold phoenix flower* buttercup

　　　　　　　　　金木犀「金・ 鳳・ 花」金鳳花

gold export pure gold silence of gold　　金輸出 金無垢 沈黙は金

gold leaf autumn breeze gold field　　　金箔 金風 金産地

gold work gold seal gold mounting　　　金工 金印 金台

close friendship gold ball testicles　　　金石変 金玉 金玉

firmness gold-cased gold brocade　　　　金鉄 金側 金襴

gold lacquer binding hand and foot gold-plated　　金蒔絵 金縛 金着

gold furniture gold doors rolled in gold　金器 金帳 かぶれ金

gold letters gold paper bundle of money　金字 金紙 金包

gold mine goldsmith iron smell　　　　　金山 金工 金臭

rust emery powder hacksaw　　　　　　　金錆 金剛 金鋸

skewer golden hairpin shears　　　　　　金串 金簪 金鋏

gold-beater castration something very cold　　金箔屋 金切 金氷

goldfish seller gold reserves prove gold　金魚屋 金準備 金の品質を.

II Sawa 二 沢

Blessing	沢
a great many	沢山
abundance	沢山
plenty	沢山
swamp	沢
marsh	沢
marshy land	沢地
swamp water	沢水
rice fields	沢田
lowlands	沢
valley	沢
flooded rice fields	沢田
a great quantity	沢山
huge radish	沢庵
pickled daikon	沢庵
edge of a swamp	沢辺

III Kana & Sawa 三 金 ＊ 沢

swamp gold	沢金
marsh gold	沢金
the rice fields flooded	沢田
ground strewn with gold dust	金地
mountain fortress	金山
gold stream	金沢

Edo

1600 - 1867

For Kanazawa, the Edo period constitutes
a flowering of aesthetic pursuits—
gold leaf
ceramics
lacquer
silk
tea
Noh,

all balanced on the overflowing rice tributes from land
gripped by the firm if ruthless hand of the Maeda clan.
Things haven't changed, so much that Kanazawa (golden
bog)
is now completely water-logged,

a place where only carp and lilies live,
reserved, traditional, conservative.

Miss Koto

Behind the strings of silk at tuning time,
the black-gowned whiplash madam looms to fork out
failure. Miss Koto prepares to swipe hard
at the strings—in time or out of favour.
She and her dozen sisters have practised
till their fingers bleed. She can play blindfold,
through mirrors, backwards, her koto singing
in another room. She builds wickerwork
out of fragile sticks of sound and wires
of shamisen to hold the wind and air
of shakuhachi breath inside her song:
a roll of thunder, buildings fall (bass koto),
a few bars later, there it goes again,
a touch of lightning, an embrace of rain.

Prologue To A Noh Play

for Kataribe theatre group, Kanazawa

We are the never-turning tide, the deathless ones,
who live upon the edge of time, ablaze
with song, unravelling your dreams. We catch
the hopes of those who don`t know how to wait,
and those who wait too long. The scavenging
is endless. Watch us weave from bare outlines
a peopled world the colour of a passion
that dares beat its sadness out; a woman
trapped in love so stormy it will spit tears
in your eyes. See past the end, the shipwreck
of a life, past clinging, past the driftwood
dragging on, to that forgotten moment
when illusion breaks and she can drop
her precious lifeline, far beyond her death.

wooden geta
the water quivers with carp
a horizon of lilies

shining through the eye slots
of the mask the player wears
the light of someone other

The Taihen Dancer

no hands

to turn the menu up
to lift his glass
and toast us
we must go to him

he hates it
snaps at my help
cuts me to the quick
I feel like running

but

    when dancing
    each foot is placed
    upon the careful earth, precisely
    as an angel would, shattering
    not a single flake of dust

he makes the perfect curve
god-drawn
    my eye travels the muscle of his legs
    trunk, neck and tiny arm—
    ground-breaking harmony

    his shoulder a quiet resting point
    for his lopsided partner
    he leads her turning body
    gloriously
    across the stage

and out he goes
and in he comes again
with two more beers
one tucked under his digit
one crooked beneath his neck

we argue about vegetables
raw versus cooked
amounts and boiling times
and why do Japanese price leafed tomatoes higher
than unleafed—is it the claim of freshness?

I plump for design
yes this is true he says
we do not think so
but the Japanese in general like to put
shape before taste

and head bent to table
cheek pushed against the grain
his digit shoves
another ball of rice
inside his mouth

The True Artist

'...conceals even from himself his own intent'
                              Zeami, in The Art Of Noh

The confectioner performs
with silence
and no fuss.

Attired in white cap and overalls,
he cups sweet rice paste
into wafer cases,

leaving his place occasionally
for water, and to wipe his face
of cinnabar.

His hands, active,
deft, smooth, floury
and scriptless,

his face, expressionless
—as if he isn't
in,

he shapes floppy triangles of sweet,
dough balls on sticks - pure sugar-coated
kanten, azuki, goma, mamaredo, an.

sickle moon, yellow
and black, on my way
back to the heart

writing the evening
brushstrokes on paper, barefoot
on the veranda

How to Be Indivisible

Prior to the wedding is the hardest work:
private grillings by polite detectives
to ascertain the family ancestors are not
tainted, though caste is now taboo,
by shoemakers, meat dealers, toilet cleaners.
(In the investigative trade
business is brisk before auspicious days).

When someone weds a foreigner,
relations feel relief,
for, once the first shock is overcome,
what worse fate can befall?
No need to fear a furtive skeleton,
whatever's found out now won't figure in tradition,
no secret past to circumvent at all.

Social positions sorted, in the wedding complex
things go smooth as silk:
the darling bride trips in upon
the right auspicious day,
arm in the groom's, feet on the edge of geta wedges
turned inward charmingly, kimono trailing,
into the shrine-room with her relatives

(and also me—
I, being foreign,
am most politely asked to tag along).

Shrine maidens circle a shinto-costumed holy man
who waves a paper wand over our heads
(mostly mine) to expel the evil spirits.

Another pair opts for the chapel, purpose-built,
in state inside the room next door—
an exclusive wedding package
that provides altar and part-time priest
(not really priest, more robed-up commoner)
for a 'romantic white'
of western wedding rite.

Whatever. Afterwards
both bridal groups
withdraw to different banquet halls,
details of decoration
pushing perfection.
Brides and grooms get up and bow,
sit down, stand up and bow again.

The wedding clothes are changed from white to red,
the feasts are savoured,
greetings given, speeches said
(first censored for any 'separating' words:
no 'break', no 'split', no 'sawn in half', no 'sundered'),
as previously proffered money gifts ward off divorce,
uncut and indivisible, odd-numbered.

Wood Song

one dragon stretched along the ground:
paulownia wood, wrested from China,
refined, lengthened and standardised,
its grainy swirls studded with 13 ji bridges;
its slim back longer than the player
(her hair in silver pins,
her kimono so tightly wound
it makes the stomach blue);
strings coiled by the tail;
air waiting.

   two schools—the round
   and the square: students of one
   sit knees straight at the koto;
   she, of the other school,
   must view the spread
   from a more delicately placed slant.

    three ivory picks,
     tsume, false nails, dragon's claws,
     divide the air
     and flit back home.

one
  two
   three—

      she sits, she kneels,
      she bows before she plays,
      tapping to give the time;
      the teachers are strict
      (blows bring out talent),
      the score traditionally
      unwritten.

Fingers slot behind the silken koto strings.

The music flies and an ivory nail
slips in between two of the thirteen ji
and picks at the wood

the paulownia sings

Vermeer Antique Shop, Kanazawa

for Masuo

Bath in the kitchen,
dust in the cupboards,
front room full of light.

Opening time is
unbrushed, sleepy-eyed.
Closing is when the customers decide.

He sells antique English glass,
hoards Dutch art books, gathers stones,
and calls his pockets empty.

I'm lazy for someone Japanese,
unlike you English
who call nearly nothing 'work'.

For hours on end, he polishes his jewels
to the piano music of Shostakovitch
or reads piecemeal from his books.

Sometimes, he simply smokes
amidst his treasures,
mind elsewhere.

At night he teaches English in the back,
refills his pipe, or sketches lizards' eggs,
line after line.

In earthquakes,
he lies calm under the futon,
and contemplates a factory job.

Gone now on a shopping trip to Europe,
he has left ghosts
to do the caretaking.

Dancing, tilting
in their light,
his shop slips nearly out of sight.

Mr Mori's Report

Everything is upside down in England.
They print books from back to front, they serve soup
for starters, they overcook fish, they eat
mushrooms raw, on Valentine's the women
receive chocolates from the men, they limit
drinking hours, they put their soapy bodies
in the bath and drain it daily, they keep
futons on the floor on stands, they never
sleep next to the blanket, and happily
set their heads towards the north, for breakfast
they do not take rice or seaweed for which
they have just one word, they use umbrellas
only when it rains. But apples are cheap,
you can eat the skin, it tastes of heaven.

Catching An Occidental

Bound in a silken cage, a silken robe,
cords made from politesse,
my soft skin patted down with creams of flattery,
shadowed by smiles called The Delightful,

the faces round me tilted
to lighten up the eyes, lids widened,
indicating admired astonishment,
charm laid thickly on,

I sleep, losing all sight
of my desire to look into the darkness
where swords lie loosely tethered at the gate
and passageways grow spikes—

netted in lace of gold,
satiated with heart-stopping rice balls.

A Day For Not Doing Anything

A young crane etched in silver
bends towards the stream. He looks
a deal too thin to swallow fish.

Nature is concreted into banks
of wildlife mown down twice a year
and the new river bed is pebbled

with little waterfalls. Delight. It is
the nearest we can approximate.
I choose the furthest spot of green.

The sun burns my eyes, the mountains blue
between my knees. A man walks past,
not looking at the scenery.

Making Rasmalai In Kanazawa

Early summer and it is already 33 degrees.

I unearth Vinita's gift of rasmalai—
to be made when missing home.

Crushed cardamom seeds
in milk & melted sugar,
bubbling all the while
an old friend drapes
his arm round
someone
else.

Back in the bread basket
who cares who
is sick.

Yoghurt ferments
with good reason.

Delicious rasmalai:
remember to refrigerate before enjoying.

Yaki Imo

Ringing out—the roasted sweet potato seller's call
(these days recorded)

Y A K I I M O O O O O

the traffic an accompaniment
in this carpet-covered room.

Maybe I'll make a curry today
for one,
a carrot, an onion.
A motorbike is buzzing in the distance.

My friend left me a pitta bread
inside the fridge.
Tears fall before I start to chop and
I bless all those who do not look.
It is a cold I have,
red-eyed,
a cold.

Still the same old yaki imo call
(tape faded)
the traffic quite loud still.

YAKI IMOOOOO

hands flutter—in pink
silk, the white sleeves droop,
upon the ground, her hair

a silverfish
streaks through the dictionaries
eating my words

There Are Always Men

Take your time
when sifting through the hangers,
for there are always men.
They merely vary in design:

Nice, Nasty and Wool-Loving-Care,
Appropriate and Durable,
Dry-Clean-Me-Only, Iron-Flat-
For-Evening-Wear

(Snow White knew them all).

And should wardrobe space be limited,
the older models can be left
to languish on the floor.

I know, I've been through thousands
and am now knee-deep in garments,
wading towards the latest Mr Right,

who promises as always
to be the ultimate in fashion,
my long longed-for knight.

Equanimity

five floors up in an earthquake country
when everything starts to shake
(including me)

is the perfect place in which to test
my equanimity towards death—
not good

Death Days To Remember:
1 3 7 13 17 23 27 33 50 100

Death days are get togethers when relations get
the chance to do a thorough check
of the intimate feelings of the most bereft.

It is expected by the thirty-third
that the survivors be no longer sad,
even a little happy, almost glad.

By the fiftieth occasion
(for those died young) it should become
a straightforward celebration.

(Mostly, the hundredth day
is getting way oh way
too many generation gaps away...).

Remembering Kobe

The worst is afterwards,
departing before early light from Kyoto
on what is left of the railway line to go
as far as you can to Kobe,
packs laden with blankets, food, drink, clothes
along the cracked unrecognisable roads,
like Urashima no Ko back from his charmed palace
three hundred years too late,
and the nights turn blacker than you knew they could,
but you must walk still four hours more uphill
to what was once a Kobe university
and spend one hour of greetings *how are you?*
how many are the missing now, the dead?
handing out your gifts of clothing, comfort, bread,
before returning on land marked with holes and rubble
and no landmarks,
the worst part being the last
before the railway line is breached,
when the light runs out
and the torches fight the dark
and you struggle on alone,
trying to keep to the way,
trying to believe that there is a way
back home.

Voice Lag

*

This flat is full
of the most peculiar draughts,
shifts in the air. Things drop
with noises in the night.

I used to think
Earthquakes! Ghosts!
but now I don`t do much
except turn over.

*

In a 2-week-old *New Statesman*, journalists record the flood.

They`ve been putting sandbags round the new estate. The police
think it is about to go. The developers of Otter View, stuffed full of
BMWs, Mercs, were warned re building so close to the river, but
said that 'This is what the buyers want: a watery aspect.'

News proceeds slowly on newsprint.

Behind, a village scene by night.

In front,
the scattered
houses stand
in moving
river.

*

email is <confined to quirky snippets that delete signs of anything more deep>

*

as for the telephone THREE AM IS WHEN THEY'RE ALL AT
TEA   ON   THEIR   SIDE   IT   MIGHT   BE   DUE   TO
ASTRONOMICAL TRANSCONTINENTAL COST THE SENSE
OF DISTANCE INTENSIFIED BY VOICE LAG MISSING
WORDS WHICH ONE SIDE NOT HEARING INTERRUPTS
FOR ME IT IS THE COUGH MY MUM MAKES ASSURING
ME SHE'S FINE WHICH GROWS IN MY STRUGGLE WITH
THE EARLY HOUR TO PNEUMONIC PROPORTIONS

*

But the nearest that I feel
to being anywhere
is when I crouch
over the squat-hole
in the floor
of an old Japanese-style caff,
a long drop beneath,
and me knowing exactly
where I sit.

*

53

watching the breath come
and go, who am I but
a broken bit of star?

Harvest

TV weather. Kanazawa. The leaves are burning
red. Some fall. It was so windy yesterday.
Two postal workers in the States expire.
Voiceover soft. On camera dolphins play.

I turn it off. Outside the water runs
along the pavement cracks. Damp maple leaves.
And empty seats flank each side of the bus.
The rain mounts with me, caught inside my sleeve.

I reach my office, flip the computer on—
two more anthrax cases diagnosed,
plug in my hotpot, rinse out last night's cup.
The sun just makes it through my dirty windows.

Elsewhere, retaliation. Terrified,
the field mice run, thin, with my brother's eyes.

The Festival Of The Dead

Lost in the hills behind Toyama,
Yatsuo, village of black sticks,
stilts, the scarecrow dance.

Three shamisen players
walk in time to the sound
of their own wooden flip-flops.

A young boy bows the kokyu,
onlookers treading his shadow.
His song floats past the wooden shutters:

The rice flowers are blooming.
Oh protect us, this Kaze no Bon,
from the season of winds.

yes

an apple plucked straight
from a branch in Nagoya—
a cricket's song

The Most Beautiful

for Yukari

coming weary from the goldstream

    dead ends every where

to the west capital

    maple temples burning
    red in the mixing bowl

    eight thousand four hundred
    taxi drivers hunt the kerb

and you pick out the local guy

    the one that doesn't make up stories
    the one that knows where to find
    the most beautiful tree

over at the palace
down by the gate
he says

    you can't miss it

Eiheiji

deep into the mountain
temple of eternal peace
and summer tourists

early morning mist
the scent of burning cedar
sweeps the moss

pine roots
spilling over
the temple steps

each day an echo
monks stepping on the polished wood
the tourists' clatter

neatly arranged shoes
around the meditation hall
neatly arranged minds

below the monk-guide shouts
head bent and motionless
a stick insect

in the autumn breeze
red leaves upon the mountain
a kimono flows

The First Fountain Ever Placed In A Japanese Garden

for my mother

more than half
is the sound of it
as it splashes on the stone rim

this is the part
the thousands of photographs
will never reach

their takers stop
to make a frieze
and then move on

no chance of hearing
the other half
clapping its moving shadow in the trees

the shudder
when the leaves
follow the foam

which drops, unmoved
as if thrown by a boy
to fall through air

diluting
dissolving
into parts

Yuki-tsuri Day

The bamboo path curves upwards. The maple leaves
have just been touched by autumn.
My favourite teahouse is closed,
the house I want to live in forever.
Gold scatters on the eaves, the roof,
the stone lantern and the doorstep.
The carp swim colourlessly
in the lake, gaping for food.

Eight men in uniform—brown, turquoise, blue
tie ropes around a pole for Yuki-tsuri Day.
In the upper teahouse, the hostess talks of snow—
expected this year in the Twelfth Month.
When she leaves, the room fills with low voices
of men at work, birds, wind, the water's sound
and the clinking of the Eiffel-tower
ladders, the rustle of ropes of straw.

The Leaf-Turning Month

Heian lady (actually Korean)
Mistress of the Robes
with Chinese cello

lit up
in the tearoom
over Misty Pond

plays
in red silk
to cameras

whiffs of sake
business suits
walk past

plastic
round the yuki-tsuri-topped
Karasaki pine—

prepared
far too early
for winter

a prime spot
for cameras
and picture postcards

crowds pass
they bother
then they stop

the music
circles, miked
over the water

Kenroku en
perfect reflection
of a perfect park

If I Were A Kimono Maker

If I were a kimono maker
searching for
a gentle swirling print
to grace the winter season,
I would go
in November,
on the last weekend
for autumn leaves,
to Gifu prefecture,
first spending the night
in an old house
of wood and paper
and hundred-year old beams
around a fire
with mountaineers,
fish cooking
on sticks made
from new-cut bamboo,
gingko nuts roasting
with mountain potato
wild mushroom,
and then,
after a few hours'
woodsmoke-filled sleep
on the tatami straw
and a warming breakfast
of sweet okayu porridge,
I would begin the climb
through the scented clearings
of cut cedar—
some still yellow,
some gone grey—

on Kogasan mountain ridge,
along which are scattered,
ready to haul the climbers up
as we clamber past
the Gifu skyline
to the peak,
the slender trunks
of the ryobu tree,
with its multi-coloured
warm grey, soft fawn
and lightest sky-blue bark,
just perfect
for my daughter's
first kimono.

Climbing

for my father

Light changes
and the green turns blue turns purple-grey
and all the land we walked on
becomes sea

The mountain is an island
so very like a whale and we
sprawled on its back
talking past lives
of happiness of pain
all come and gone
chill to the bone
the weather soaking in
until thin plastic becomes
just not enough
and we must walk again
across the flinty fields of rain

Tantalus

Clothed in cloud,
feathered heights,
who could resist?

The mountain path curls up
but what seems summit
poking through the autumn grasses
is more hill.

A dawn of mountain bell flowers,
pale petals,
beetles climb over the nut
dropped from the hanging tree,

a mahiwa sings highly
of nothing
and grains of sand shift
underneath the boulders.

An ant pushes past
the tall green blades
to hurtle forwards,
crushing tinier worlds.

At the peak
mere shrouds of cloud,
spirals of water-drops,
a wind that moans,
wills in the wisp.

Hakusan Mountain Scenes

I

Rucksacks cling to the wall
and five worn-in pairs
of climbing boots
track along the bookcase,
which contains ridge
upon ridge of mountain
photographs and maps,
neatly stacked, with cairns
of undeveloped film.

II

Save for a touch of green,
the mist is washed of colour
and branches stretch out
where they drop,
supine.

III

Mori rolls over in the mountain hut,
first negotiating with his neighbour's ribs.
Like sardines, forced to share dreams.
There is a smell of fish.

Packed tightly into damp rows
of pin-width mattresses,
only the green-eyed gaijin
gets two slots—overgrown foreigner.

Some prefer to haul their tents,
tent-poles and pegs, gas-ring
and chopsticks, plate and cup, noodles
the two thousand four hundred and forty metres up.

Mori's feet are sore. His upper neighbour snores.
Today there is no 4 am fair-weather drum,
no sunrise climb, no view.
No sleep for Mori.

But outside, breathless in their clouds
around the hut and piled above it
hanging upon the peak, swirl crowds
of unseen, lonely gods.

Cloud And Crane

How can I ever be one
with you who call me
gaijin, outside person

    Oh how I envy your inability
    to be anything
    other than different

you who were taught
to prize above all
the skill of being the same

    you who simply
    fail to notice
    the chasm you create

hammering down
the peg that dares
stick out

    by not anticipating my need
    for furo, meshi, neru
    bath, dinner, sleep

drifting
mountains shoulder the sky
blotches of pine

Up To The Hilt

The snow falls like it used to
in the olden days,
when the samurai would ring to cancel,
stuck, or fearing to be soaked
up to the buttocks
in snow drift,

and my carefully-sewn-together day unravels
into threads of futon,
unread magazines, banana skins
and little jobs, while whatever apology
of vegetables remains
is snipped into survival soup.

Needless activities abound—
bouts of coffee,
tea-drinking,
lounging around, slices
of television, sword-polishing,
anything.

No one that matters is about,
and the only sound,
save for an occasional helicopter-whirr
of snow plough,
is that of carving cake—
shops engaging local warriors
in snow removal.

Midwinter

One breath
beyond the muffled
silence, and
from somewhere
comes floating
the fragrance
of a hyacinth,

light,
unexpected in the snow.

The Weight Of Things

At Ishikawa Prefectural Museum
of Art, my pocket fills with keys
from lockers and umbrella stands
where I have placed
a yellow bag of heavy vegetables;
one classic manga book, now out of print;
a convenience-store, three-hundred-yen umbrella,
worth its weight in rainy weather;
and my purse, bursting with discarded business cards.

I am already wearing holes
in my silk jacket—
all that loose change
keeps sneaking out, *clink clink.*
The ticket girl looks up
so I pay for the cheap,
the permanent exhibition,
three hundred and fifty—
more than my umbrella,

to behold a flawless seventeenth century ko-kutani bowl
'shallow with design of tree'
in ocean green and trunk of brown;
soft orange fills the centre,
the rim lined with the same aquatic green.

There is a postcard of it, smaller,
priced at fifty yen.
I buy it, neatly packaged,
to look at in the cafe
where they sell two-centimetre
hunks of toasted bread at two hundred and fifty,
and cheese cake, either rare or baked,
sliced small, for an enormous price
(with tea it comes to two umbrellas).

As I unwrap my postcard,
the clientele all crowd onto one side,
tipping the cafe towards the windows
that reach down to the floor, and up
into the trees.

Nearly Nowhere

We reach a place
where I could never go alone,
a cliff face,

a place that looked at is not there,
where love thickens and then vanishes,
a place the crows wing by.

You show me the poem
I conceived last night
already printed in a book.

I talk of mountains you have climbed.
You plan the future
that I had in mind.

Minds meet but too polite
we turn away our heads,
the likeness frightening.

Driving To Noto

Men are better says Toshi I know
no they are not says I (I also know)
and so we argue to the tip of Noto

To Suzu where the wood huts slump in shock
plopped suddenly in frocks of snow
and the sea is whipped to icicles of frenzy

Over a nabe pot of fish and cabbage
(Toshi warns me not to call it cabbage
for it is the vastly superior hakusai)
our host asks me my age

Taken aback
(I'm older than he thought
more single), he inquires
don't you like men?

So I assure him
only frequent country-moving
has prevented me from choosing
one of them

The returning road is white, wide as a field
the ditches spread themselves with frosting
and the windscreen blanks out like a blizzard

Toshi scrapes at the iced-up wipers singing
to himself, waving me in

Midwinter hangs in the boughs

The pine trees are bent nearly in two
laden with second helpings

yes

crammed in the cafe
knees bumping, our heads
in a crick as they turn
to catch titbits of chat

you her friend? says
a friend and my
not-yet-friend
freezes

his whole frame on pause
ringing up
the significances, tumbling
walls, to answer him

yes

Glossary of Japanese

Most of the Japanese words and characters are placed next to their English equivalents. For the curious, a few are also included here.

kanten, azuki, goma, mamaredo, an—ingredients of traditional sweets
ah sososo—oh I see
daikon—a type of large radish
furo, meshi, neru—bath, dinner, sleep (the proverbial utterances of a traditional Japanese husband to his wife)
gaijin—literally 'outside person', non-honorific word for foreigners from the West
geta—traditional footwear, similar to flip-flops with a thicker sole
Kaze no Bon—the Wind Festival of the Dead
kita—north
kokyu—a Chinese cello-like instrument
ko-kutani—old-style porcelain from Kutani village in Kaga
koto—a harp-like instrument, played on the ground
mahiwa—siskin songbird
manga—comic book
sake—an alcoholic drink made from rice
shakuhachi—an end-blown bamboo flute
shamisen—a three-stringed lute
Shinto—the indigenous religion of Japan
suu suu guusuka - zzzzzzz (the sound of snoring)
tadaima—I'm home
taihen—too much or extremely, also the name of a Japanese group of dancers with disabilities; tai can mean 'appearance, figure', and hen, 'change'
yaki imo—roasted sweet potato
yukata—informal summer kimono
yuki-tsuri - snow net supports for trees
ええ ee—yes

羽 hane—wings

金沢 Kanazawa—city in Ishikawa prefecture, Japan

喜 yoroko(bi) —joy